DEEP INTO THE MARKETS

Making Sales for Business Growth and Profits

Harris K. Engstrom

COPYRIGHT

All rights reserved. No part of this publication may be reproduced, distributed, or transmitted in any form or by any means, including photocopying, recording or other electronic or mechanical method, without the prior written permission of the publisher, except in the case of brief quotation embodied in critical review and certain other noncommercial uses permitted by copyright law.

Copyright © Harris K. Engstrom, 2024.

About the book

Deep into the Markets is an exceptional book that *teaches how to master strategies and techniques of the 'markets' in terms of sales and marketing, so as to grow and make profits*. Whether you are a business owner, a sales manager, a salesperson, or a marketer, this book will provide you with the concepts, tools, and techniques that will help you achieve your sales and marketing goals and objectives.

In this book, you will learn:

- How to develop effective strategies to boost sales and also expand business.
- Build customer trust and loyalty by delivering value and quality.
- Increase your brand awareness and reputation by creating and communicating your unique value proposition.

- Become competitive and be able to differentiate yourself from your rivals by leveraging your strengths and opportunities.
- Manage and motivate sales team to perform at their best.

This book is based on the latest research and best practices from the fields of sales, marketing, psychology, and economics. It also features case studies and examples of successful businesses that have gone deep into the markets and achieved remarkable results.

Deep into the Markets *is more than just a book.* It is a guide, a mentor, and a partner that will accompany you on your journey to success.

About the Author

Harris K. Engstrom is an award-winning author, entrepreneur, and educator who write about business, marketing, leadership and innovation. He covers a wide range of topics, from the basics of business and marketing to the latest trends in innovation.

He provides real-world examples, case studies, and best practices. He also offers actionable advice and tips on how to apply the concepts and tools he presents. Harris's books are practical, engaging and inspiring.

Harris is always eager to connect with his readers and learn from them. He believes that life is a journey of learning and discovery, and that writing is a way of sharing his journey with others.

When he is not writing, teaching, or speaking, he enjoys reading, traveling, and listening to music

Don't miss this opportunity to learn from one of the best in the field. Buy Harris's books today and discover how to succeed in business and innovation.

some insightful books by same author:
- **The Great Business Founders**
- **The Versatile Hands**
- **The Business with Future Strings**

TABLE OF CONTENT

About the book 3

INTRODUCTION 10

CHAPTER 1 13

    Sales and marketing strategy 13
    strategy to boost sales 19
        Understanding competitive advantage and market niche. 20
        Case study 24

.... **Error! Bookmark not defined.**

CHAPTER 3 29

    Selection of the Profitable Strategy 29
    Sales and Sales forecast 41
    Techniques to boost Sales and Profits 49

CHAPTER 5 63

The power of collaboration in business 63

CHAPTER 6 67

Executing Effective Sales and Marketing Plan 67
Implementing the Sales Strategy 75
    sales strategy for sales team 78
    Effective Strategies to close deal and make sales 80
    Case Study 88

CHAPTER 8 93

Management of the Sales Department 93
    Creation of sales process and sales pipeline 94

CHAPTER 9 103

Getting Customers Trust and Loyalty 103
Tips to promote your product and its popularity 105

Sales innovation for offerings 106
Measuring Your Sales 109
Case Study 112

CONCLUSIONS 118

INTRODUCTION

'The Market' as a place for business, is a very complex and dynamic environment that provides both opportunities and competition to businesses. To be successful in the markets, your business needs to understand the needs and wants of your customers, behavior and preferences of competitors and the trends in the environment. To succeed require you enter *'deep' into its markets.* This simply means creating and implementing effective sales and marketing strategies, targeting the most profitable and attractive businesses that can give you that edge. It also means measuring sales and marketing results as well as making adjustments when necessary. The main purpose of going *deep into the market*s is to achieve growth and profitability for business expansion and the future.

To enter deep into the markets, companies must:

1. *Identify and meet customers' unmet needs, creating value and loyalty.*
2. *Gain competitive advantage and differentiate themselves from competitors by creating value and awareness.*
3. *Seize new opportunities and overcome new threats to create growth and innovation.*
4. *Improve resources and processes to create efficiency and effectiveness.*

This book will guide you through the process of delving deeper into the markets. You will learn strategics, tools and techniques that will help you achieve your sales and marketing goals. You'll also learn best practices and case studies from successful business that have dug deep into their business and achieved significant results.

CHAPTER 1

Sales and marketing strategy

Every organization success is dependents on its growth and expansion. This growth is only possible when the sales numbers are also good. To succeed with sales depends largely on the marketing and Sales plan. This chapter covers what it takes to gets there.

To develop your sales and marketing strategies :

Define your sales goals and metrics to align with your business goals.

- *Identify target markets and customers based on region, industry, size, sales, etc. and categorize them by factor.*
- *Provide feedback to your salespeople to help them improve their sales skills and performance.*

- *Adjust and rebalance your space as needed based on changes in the market, customer behavior or sales.*
- *Prospect by identify and qualify customers who might buy from you.*
- *Research your prospects and understand their needs, goals, and pain. Points.* Use email, phone calls, social media, etc. to reach your potential customers'

Use different methods.

- *Create a personal and valuable message that will capture the attention and interest of potential customers.*
- *Use tools like LinkedIn Sales Navigator to find and qualify leads and tools like Hub Spot Sales to optimize and improve your presentation.*

- *Qualify potential customers by determining whether they are potential customer or not.*

Ask yourself, whether they are suitable for your product or service? And do they have the energy, budget and speed to buy from you?

- *Listen carefully and patiently to the vision, draw conclusions, and make sure you understand the problem. Use appropriate methods such as (Budget, Responsibilities, Needs, Time) or (Measurement, Business Process, Decision-Making, Decision-Making Process to evaluate products ready for purchase.*
- **Demonstrate to** *show how your products or services solve your customers' problems and create value for them.*
- *Negotiate the terms of the contract with the customer and try to reach an agreement.*

Negotiations techniques

Build relationships and trust with potential customers and focus on creating value rather than cutting costs. Improve decision-making processes and procedures and address their concerns and expectations.

Use SPIN (Situation, Question, Alert, and Need-Reward) technology to identify your prospects' pain points and highlight their benefits. Create and submit professional proposals and contracts.

Close the Deal to finalize with your prospects and get them to sign the contract and make the payment.

Best practices for closing are:

Confirm your prospects' commitment and satisfaction, then summarize the value and benefits of the deal. Ask for the sale directly and confidently and use closing techniques such as the assumption close, the urgency close or the trial close.

Following up and follow through with your prospects. Overcome any last-minute objections or hurdles.

In addition;

Plan, rehearse, and adapt your presentation to your specific needs and goals. Use narrative and visuals to bring your vision to life and demonstrate the benefits. Manage complaints and inquiries safely and efficiently, providing evidence and documentation to support your claims. Use tools like Zoom or Google Meet for online meetings and presentations if possible.

CHAPTER 2

strategy to boost sales

There is the need to first, align your sales goals and metrics with your business objectives. After the goals, segment your target market and customers based on criteria such as geography, industry, size, revenue, etc.

Assign your sales reps to the most suitable territories based on their skills, experience, and performance. Use data and analytics to evaluate your territory potential, coverage, and penetration. Adjust and balance your territories as needed to account for changes in market conditions, customer behavior, or sales performance. After that, define your sales process and identify the key stages and activities involved.

Choose the sales metrics and KPIs that reflect your sales performance and objectives.

Use tools and methods to collect and visualize your sales data, such as spreadsheets, CRM solutions, or data analytics platforms. Finally, analyze your sales data and look for patterns, trends, and insights that can help you understand your sales performance and identify areas of strength and weakness. Implement changes and improvements based on your sales analysis, and monitor the impact and results of your actions

Understanding competitive advantage and market niche.

Competitive advantage may be based on price, quality, innovation, customer service or other aspects of your business. Business loyalty programs can help companies increase business, profitability and customer loyalty and as a result gain competitive advantage.

A niche market is a segment of a larger market with specific needs, interests or personalities. Marketing niches can be defined based on criteria such as geography, demographics, income, interests, or behaviors. *Niche marketing can help companies focus on smaller, more targeted customers and avoid direct competition with larger, more established businesses.*

Niche competitive advantage is the competitive advantage gained by participating in a niche market and serving it better than other markets. Niche competitive advantages can help companies differentiate themselves from competitors and create value for customers.

Niche competitive advantage can be achieved by using one or more of the following strategies:

- Offer unique products or services that meet specific customer needs or needs
- Provide better performance, efficiency or reliability than existing alternatives on the market.

- Offer lower or better prices than competitors.

Studies on activities that resulted in competitive advantages in some businesses.

- A store that specializes in pencils, scissors, books and other products for lefties. Lefties are niche market often overlooked by major retailers and has a wide range of products that meet their specific needs.
- Netflix: The streaming service offers a wide and diverse selection of movies, TV shows, documentaries and original content. Netflix targets a niche market of entertainment seekers who like to watch content based on TV series. Netflix also uses data and personal information to customize recommendations and create content tailored to customer interests.

- Lush a cosmetics company that produces and sells handmade, natural and ethical products such as soaps, shampoos, bath bombs and more.

Lush's business mission is to be environmentally conscious and responsible for consumers who care about the ingredients, packaging and quality of personal care products. Lush also engages consumers through storytelling, action and community engagement.

Case study

Sales Collaboration among Partners.

Sampled business collaboration between different industries and businesses and their outcomes.

1. **The RAMP Sports and C4 Waterman.**

A partnership agreement of two complementary products with a shared sustainability benefit. RAMP Sports is a ski company that produces eco-friendly skis and snowboards, and C4 Waterman is a paddleboard company that uses recycled and recyclable materials.

The two companies merged to cross-sell products to each other's customers and extended sales seasons year-round. They also coordinated marketing campaigns, events and social media to increased product awareness and customer loyalty. Through joint sales, both companies expanded sales, customer base, and market share.

2. **_Salesforce and Google_**

These are examples of two sales technology companies working together to provide solutions and services to their customers. *Salesforce is a leading cloud CRM platform and Google is a leading search engine and online advertising provider.*

The two companies have joined forces to provide customers with a comprehensive and powerful combination of CRM, analytics and productivity tools.

They also offer incentives and discounts to customers who sign up for platforms, as well as training and support to help customers market most of their decisions.

Through joint sales, both companies increase their offerings, customer satisfaction and competitive advantage.

3. *Affiliate and Large Financial Services Firm*

This is also an example of affiliate marketing between an outsourcing sales firm and a large financial services firm to create new products and write market research.

Affiliate Marketing is a company that specializes in delivering customized and scalable products to clients of one of the world's largest business, insurance and investment providers. The two companies have partnered on a large-scale commercial venture that involves the distribution and collection of research data from small and medium-sized businesses in the United States.

Affiliate marketing provides sustainable financial services with a team of trained and qualified salespeople who use technology to track and report their activities and benefits.

As a result of the joint venture, the financial services company successfully developed new products, achieved valuable business results, and increased leads and sales.

These case studies demonstrate how some sales partnerships have helped companies achieve their goals and objectives by leveraging partners' strengths, resources, and networks.

CHAPTER 3

Selection of the Profitable Strategy

To excel in the market will require the implementation of effective and profitable strategies. Let delve into some effective strategies you can adopt for your sales and marketing team.

Price-based selling:

This sales strategy *focuses on the price and value of a product or service that can be offered to customers, rather than its features.* This can help you build trust with your customers and prove your value.

An example of a company using wholesale pricing is UPS, which offers a variety of shipping options and solutions to meet customer needs.

Inbound marketing: This is a marketing strategy that attracts and educates customers by providing valuable and relevant content such as blogs, e-books, videos, and more. This can help you generate, qualify and increase sales. HubSpot is an example of an inbound marketing company that provides rich content and resources to help customers learn and grow.

Inbound sales are about attracting customers interested in your product or service and incentivizing them through sales. You use online content, such as blogs, e-books, and webinars, to provide information and value to your customers and gain trust. You can also use tools like social media, email marketing and more to increase your online exposure and visibility.

Inbound sales are more customer-focused because you focus on solving their problems and meeting their needs.

But inbound sales can also take more time because you have to create and distribute good content and wait for people to find you and contact you. An internal sale requires more cooperation and collaboration between marketing and sales as they must work together to create, qualify, and move products to the sales stage.

Outbound sales *occur when you attract customers who have not yet purchased your product, show interest in your product or service, and encourage them to buy from you.* You can use cold calling, email marketing, direct mail, and more to connect with customers and sell your products.

Manage and improve your sales process with tools like CRM, sales automation, support documentation and more. *An outbound sale is more about sales because it focuses on finding and closing sales.* Selling outside your company is also more profitable because you can find and target the best and manage the sales cycle.

But outside sales can also be more expensive because you spend more money on marketing materials and products. Outside sales also requires additional skills and training, because you must overcome resistance and rejection and meet expectations.

Outside selling brings more competition and excitement as you compete with other sellers for leadership and profit. The best sales strategy for your business depends on your business goals.

points to consider:

If you offer a good product or service, you will need external vendors who will share and promote your vision, sales and products with them for a long time. If you offer a simple or low-cost product or service, you can use marketing to attract and convert leads and increase sales. If you are targeting a specific market or niche, you will need an external service provider to identify and reach your target audience.

Use the right products and trade accordingly.

If you focus on general marketing, you can use marketing strategies to generate leads, qualify leads, and distribute sales. If your sales cycle is long or difficult, you will need a sales team to meet potential customers and direct them to the sales phase. If your sales cycle is short or simple, you can easily generate leads and increase sales. There is no single answer to what type of sale is right for your business. The best way to decide is to evaluate both strategies and see which one provides the best results for your business. You can mix the two strategies and enjoy the results of each. For example, you can use inbound sales to generate leads and outbound sales to close them.

Alternatively, you can use international sales for cold metal work and domestic sales for hot metal work. It's important to align sales with your business and marketing goals and continually measure and improve sales.

Increasing sales by attracting more potential customers is a goal for many businesses. *A lead is a potential customer who has shown interest in your product or service and has the potential to convert into a paying customer.*

There are a variety of ideas and strategies to reach more potential customers, including: Share great content that educates, entertains, and solves problems with your audience. Content can include blog posts, eBooks, videos, podcasts, info graphics, and more. You can use content to demonstrate your expertise, build trust, and drive traffic to your website. Create a lead magnet that offers value to your prospects in exchange for their contact information. Lead magnets can include free trials, tests, discussions, coupons, reviews, tips, and more. You can use lead magnets to attract customers and increase your email number. Improve the application to guide customers. The text should be clear, simple, and easy to write.

All you have to do is to ask for the most basic information, such as your name, email address, and phone number. You can also use a call to action to encourage your audience to take action. Use SEO (Social Engine Optimization) and social media marketing to increase your online visibility and influence. SEO helps you rank higher in search engines and drives organic traffic to your website or landing page. A marketing plan can help you reach your audience, share content, and generate great ideas. Marketing strategies can help increase customer retention, lower churn, and increase conversions. Conduct webinars and demos to showcase your product or service and demonstrate its value. Webinars and demos can help educate prospects, address pain points, and overcome resistance. Webinars and briefings can also help drive conversation, develop policy, and receive feedback.

Create interactive content and landing pages that engage your audience and motivate them to take action. Interactive content and landing pages can include quizzes, surveys, calculators, games, and more.

Interactive content and landing pages help you engage, share, and personalize your content. Improve the customer experience of your website and provide your potential customers with a smooth and enjoyable browsing experience.

How to increase sales in the markets.
Track sales and marketing:

Set goals with your sales and marketing team. You need to enable your sales and marketing teams to collaborate and share information, ideas, and resources. You need to set clear, measurable and measurable goals for both groups and align them with your business goals.

Choose sales and marketing strategy. Reach and engage your target customers through email, social media, SEO, content marketing, webinars, cold calling and more. You should choose the best methods and strategies: You should try to optimize your marketing and advertising plans. You should focus on sales and marketing and complete your actions and strategies according to your time and money. Progress and performance must be monitored and measured.

Evaluate and improve sales and marketing results. You should analyze your sales and marketing data to identify patterns, trends, and insights that will help you understand your sales and marketing and identify your strengths and weaknesses. As an analyst, you will implement the changes and improvements as well as monitor the impact and results of your work.

Create a sales plan.

A sales plan defines your business' sales goals to ensure business success and performance. It can also help you define your goals; including how much of each product, service, or experience you need to sell and how you'll achieve those sales. Customer needs and purchases should be included in the sales plan you create for your business. Focus on your sales and set goals for your sales team. Measuring your team's performance against these goals is critical to ensuring your business is profitable. Share your business goals with your team. Many business owners refuse to share information. If your employees don't understand what you want them to strive for, it will be difficult for them to understand the specific goals you want to achieve.

Business goals you want to achieve may include:

- How to achieve a leadership position.
- Manage the business to achieve sales goals.
- Open a "brand" in your niche that expands into new areas by marketing your products or services.
- Then target each goal, showing the steps you've planned

Examples of these steps include:
Providing of specific training to your employees to ensure they have knowledge and skills related to your products. Inform your team about your business goals, your business, or the specific area you want to focus on when writing down your sales activities to your sales team. This should happen every day or every week; for example, a phone call, email or in-person visit. It is recommended that you ask your sales team to record or document their achievements against the goals you set.

Your sales plan should end with an explanation of how you will measure the effectiveness of your efforts, not only by increase in total sales but also by increase in traffic sales and visit conversion. The Sales objectives define the sales objectives of the business to ensure business success and performance.

Use a sales plan to define your goals, including how much of each product, service, or experience you want to sell and how you will achieve those sales.

> **Sales increase**

Sales and Sales forecast

A sales forecast is an estimate of the sales you expect to achieve over a longer period of time (e.g. monthly, quarterly, annually). The Sales Forecast uses your sales history or market research to support each forecast.

Forecasts can be listed by product or and segment. It is important to make realistic predictions. This includes: how many new customers you gain and how many you lose each year. Average sales refer to the number of customers you gain or lose each month, the number of products you sell in a year, or the number of sales you make in a year or month in your business class. Or the monthly sales limit you want to reach by segment. Write your sales forecast into your business plan.

Sales goals are the number of products you need to sell over a specific period of time to break even or make a profit.

These goals should align with your business plan. Successful sales teams strive to achieve sales goals that are clearly defined in their training programs and sales plans. Track incentives and bonuses to keep you motivated and rewarded. It's a good idea to continuously measure, compete, and improve your sales performance. Effective Sales Goals track sales growth over time and adjust sales goals to fit your business and marketing needs. You can set goals for each segment, region, or each member of your sales team. Your sales target is part of your sales plan and is used to achieve your business's financial performance plan to generate profits and ensure the long-term sustainability of your business.

Setting the Sales Goals

Setting sales goals need to be Specific and realistic.

Use a sales plan to define your goals, including the quantity of each product, service, or information you want to sell and how you will achieve those sales.

A sales plan defines the sales objectives of the business to ensure good marketing and good results.

Help your sales team performs confidently, consistently, and gain a clear understanding of your prospects. Choosing the right goals and involving your team in choosing those goals can help you reach your sales goals and increase your profits.

Targeting each product is an easy and successful way to achieve your monthly sales budget. Sales goals typically indicate how many products you need to sell and the average sales target you need to generate revenue.

Successful sales can be achieved by clearly defining sales goals for each division and customer. The 80:20 rules are an important sales planning rule. Also known as the Pareto Principle, this principle generally means that you *get 80% of your revenue from 20% of your customers*. Research your business and identify a 20% profit margin that will help you set and achieve your sales goals.

Market segmentation (or market segmentation) is a good starting point for setting effective sales goals. However, setting sales goals by segment can be very difficult. Integrating a business means bringing together customers who have similar needs and characteristics and respond similarly to your product or service.

For example, a hardware store might divide its customers into two groups: home buyers and industrial. Consumer surveys are often grouped by: Geography (world region, country, state or region), Demographics (age, gender, family size, income, employment, education, health, religion, and race), Psychographics (personality, lifestyle), values, opinions).

Use your marketing plan as a guide to market your products and services based on the characteristics of your market segment to help you reach your sales goals.

Regional Stores or travel agencies often create sales goals by region, eliminating the complexity and frustration of setting and tracking goals for various products. These businesses find it easier to create a dollar plan for each region that covers all products and all customers in that region.

Note that, as your business grows your sales goals should increase as well.

A good sales plan sets goals for areas that will lead to business growth. For example, if the market is looking for compression fitness apparel, a wellness retailer will increase the targeting of that product line. When setting sales goals, consider how much money you will make from each sale (it doesn't make sense to hit a sales goal, but you will have to make less money to hit that goal). Be realistic, your goals should be supported by your business plan.

Consider and develop an operating cost growth plan and decide to sell unsold products at a lower price. Setting sales goals helps you evaluate the performance of each member of your sales team.

Setting unrealistic goals can have a negative impact on your business in a variety of ways, including motivating your salespeople. When setting goals for your team, make sure your team has sufficient training and product knowledge to achieve the goals you set.

Think about these questions together with your team

- *Who is buying this now?*
- *How much do they buy each year?*
- *Which customers are most likely to continue buying from you?*
- *What do they buy every year?*
- *Which will it be?*

Most customers will continue to buy from you. Most customers will order more.

How do you persuade customers to buy when you think they will order less and why? How many new customers do you need to maintain your current sales and reach your sales goals? What is your sales pattern each year? Is it seasonal or work-related? Most salespeople know your product well and understand how it will perform in your business. Involve them in collecting data, analyzing sales, and setting sales goals. Bring your team together to think about these questions. The more your team participates in setting sales goals, the more likely they are to achieve them. Improve sales effectiveness by analyzing sales goals to identify employee training, development, and training needs. Ask each employee what additional training they think would help increase sales. *Motivate your sales team and motivate them to achieve their goals.*

Consider offering incentives such as movie tickets, theater tickets or bonuses at the end of the month to best sales persons.

When it comes to sales goals, set specific goals for your employees, consider your sales plan, and set specific goals for your sales team. Goals are determined by the customer.

Shows how effective your sales team is at building and managing relationships with existing customers. Share the number of phone calls and in-person meetings your sales team needs to make each day or week to achieve their goals. Give them tools like spreadsheets or access to customer relationship management (CRM) to record their calls and meetings. By setting goals, you can measure performance and evaluate strengths and areas for improvement. Turn your idea into a business plan.

CHAPTER 4

Techniques to boost Sales and Profits

If you want to grow your business and increase your revenue, *you must create a good sales experience.*

A sales strategy is a plan that shows how a product or service will be sold for commercial purposes. It covers everything from cost, purpose, communication, motivation, expansion, production, development.

In this section, we'll look at proven strategies that can help you increase your sales and profits. These strategies are based on research, best practices, and real-life examples of successful businesses.

After reading this chapter, you will have a clear understanding of how to apply these strategies to your own business and achieve your sales goals.

Make sure your costs drive revenue.

Price is one of the most important factors affecting your sales and profits. If the price of your product or service is too high, you may lose customers to your competitors. If your rates are too low, you may not be able to pay your bills or make enough money.

Therefore, you must find the best price that will maximize your revenue and profit. You can do this by using pricing software or tools to analyze competitive pricing, customer needs, and business models.

This can help you set a price that reflects the value of your product or service, matches what your customers are willing to pay, and gives you a competitive advantage.

Set clear goals.

Goals are important for all sales. They help you determine what you want to achieve, measure progress, and make adjustments if necessary. Without goals, you lack motivation and direction.

Therefore, you need to set realistic and attainable sales goals for your team. To do this, *you can use SMART (Specific, Measurable, Achievable, Relevant, and Time-bound) criteria.* This can help you create goals that are clear, quantifiable, realistic, aligned with your vision, and set a date.

Communicate more with your customers.

Communication is a key to any sales strategy. It helps you build trust, loyalty and referrals with your customers and prospects. Without communication, you might miss opportunities, lose customers and damage your reputation. Therefore, you need to communicate more with your customers and prospects.

To do this, you can use various channels such as email, social media, phone, or chat to engage with them.

This can help you provide value, solve problems, answer questions, and create rapport. You can also use customer feedback and surveys to understand their needs, preferences, and pain

Create more incentives.

Motivation is the driving force behind any sales strategy. It helps you attract new customers and retain your existing customers.

Without motivation, you may struggle to develop leads, convert leads, and maintain loyalty. That's why you need to create more incentives for your customers and potential customers. You can do this by offering discounts, coupons, free trials, or a loyalty program to attract them. You can also use upselling and cross-selling strategies to increase your customer's average order value and lifetime value.

Start a new business to make a profit. Entering new markets is a great way to increase sales and profits.

It can help you attract new customers, diversify your income and reduce risk. By not entering new markets, you may limit your growth, face more competition and pursue a single market. Therefore, you need to enter new businesses to increase your profits. You can do this by expanding your reach by targeting a new area, customer group or niche market. You can also explore new ways or collaborations to increase your visibility and reach potential customers

Increase productivity.

Efficiency is important for all sales. It helps you reduce costs, save time and increase sales. Without productivity, you run the risk of wasting resources, losing productivity, and missing deadlines. Therefore, to increase your income, you need to increase your productivity.

You can do this by using automation, outsourcing, or empowerment to improve your sales process.

You can use sales software or tools to manage your leads, contacts, sales pipeline, and operations. This will help you track progress, improve performance and measure results

Continuous improvement for better results

Development is the ultimate goal of sales. It helps you learn from your mistakes, try new ideas and improve your performance. Without progress, you are likely to remain stagnant, falling behind and losing your edge.

Therefore, you should constantly improve your sales strategy to get better results. You can do this by using data and analytics to measure your sales results and identify areas for improvement. Do you want your brand to stand out in a crowded and competitive market? Do you want to attract more customers, increase sales, and grow your business?

If so, you need to use a good marketing strategy to increase awareness and influence of your business. *Brand awareness is how your target audience recognizes and remembers your brand. Brand power is the influence a brand has on a customer's thoughts, preferences, and behavior.*

Both are important for building a strong, loyal customer base and achieving your business goals. So, how do you gain business knowledge and influence in today's digital world?

There are several ways to do this, but the best ones to try are:

Social media

Social media is a powerful tool to connect with your customers and prospects. You can use it to interact with them, share content that matters to them, and promote user-generated content. This helps you build trust, authority, and word of mouth.

You can also use social media to promote your brand, values and culture and create awareness among your followers.

Employees are encouraged to leave comments to expand on the message

Your employees are your best managers. It can help you promote your brand, products and services within your network. By encouraging your employees to share your content and stories on social media channels, you can reach new audiences, increase your authority, and achieve people's goals. By rewarding your employees, you can motivate them and encourage them to be more engaged and productive.

Focus on video content

Videos are one of the most popular and popular content on the web. It helps you introduce your product or service, tell your brand's story, and connect with your target audience on an emotional level.

You can use video to show how your product or service works, solve customer problems, and improve their lives. You can use videos to showcase customer testimonials, behind-the-scenes photos, and interesting or inspiring stories about your brand.

Collaboration with influencers

An influencer is someone who has a large and loyal following on social media or other platforms. It can help you increase brand awareness, attract leads, and increase conversion rates. To find the right people for your brand, you need to consider relevance, reach, and alignment with your business goals. You need to find influencers who share your vision, vision and niche. Influencer with a large audience, create accurate and relevant content to communicates your brand in a positive way.

Win a contest or receive a gift

Contests and sweepstakes are a great way to attract attention, increase brand awareness, and grow your email list.

You can give away your products or services as a gift or partner with another brand. You can also ask members to perform specific actions, such as following your social media accounts, liking or commenting on posts, sharing content, or tagging friends. This can help you increase your social media presence, reach, and engagement. Make sure your event has clear rules, goals, and metrics, and track participants and winners.

To attract new customers to your brand, you can offer your customers incentives such as discounts, gifts, or cash. You can also make your referral program easy to use, track, and share and remind customers of the benefits of referring others.

Develop effective SEO skills

SEO stands for Search Engine Optimization, which is the process of improving a website's visibility and relevance in search engines such as Google or Bing. SEO can help you drive organic traffic, leads, and sales to your website.

To optimize your website for SEO, you need to consider factors such as keywords, content, links, speed, and user experience. You need to use relevant and popular keywords that match your customers' search intent, create high-quality and original content that provides value to your audience, build links from reputable and authoritative websites that point to your website, improve your website's loading speed and performance, and enhance your website's design and navigation to provide a positive user experience.

Partner with like-minded brands

Partnering with other brands that share your values, vision, and audience can help you expand your reach, increase your credibility, and create value for your customers. You can partner with other brands for co-branding, co-branding or cross-promotion. For example, you may partner with other brands to create and share content, host webinars or events, offer discounts or bundles, or introduce new products or services.

You can also leverage each other's audiences, connections, and resources to achieve common goals.

These are some ways to enter the market for maximum visibility and impact. By using these strategies, you can make your business profitable, memorable and profitable, ultimately growing your business and achieving your goals.

Effective techniques to achieve increase productivity in team

Encourage and motivate teamwork.

Ensure both groups have access to relevant information and encourage them to share ideas and results

Establish common key performance indicators

Collaboration is effective when everyone is working toward the same goal. Define KPI in line with your overall business goals. Make it personal. Build strong team relationships. Encourage interaction between work, group meals, and social events. Create a shared work schedule.

Create a process that encourages.

Regularly review activities, communications, and project management tools to ensure consistency. Encourage open discussion between groups to bridge gaps.

Encourage open discussion, ask questions, and collect feedback from suppliers and companies.

Both groups must be held accountable for their contributions. Collaboration thrives when everyone is accountable for shared results.

Hold regular meetings

Plan regular business meetings to discuss progress the next steps. These meetings encourage collaboration and keep everyone on the same page. Good collaboration doesn't mean working in just one way.

Working together means to share knowledge and moving forward together. Using these strategies, you can create a harmonious environment that increases sales and productivity.

CHAPTER 5

The power of collaboration in business

Sales and Marketing teams work toward common goals and collaborate effectively. These adjustments ensure that work is completed without interruption. Example, if the marketing department's goal is lead generation, the sales department can provide information about the quality of the leads and convert them into customers.

Sales and marketing teams have unique knowledge. By working together, they can develop a shared understanding of their position. Marketing can provide information about customer behavior and preferences, and sales can provide actual feedback about interactions.

When two teams work together, they can better understand the customer journey. Example Marketing can analyze customer interactions across multiple channels, and sales can provide direct information about customer pain points and problems. Collaboration makes prospecting easier. Marketing can create content and sales can drive engagement. Marketing provides educational content (like blog posts, webinars), and sales uses these resources to generate leads. Open communication between sales and marketing instead of silos and poor communication. Regular meetings or project management tools allow teams to discuss strategy, activities and progress. Collaboration encourages feedback. Teams can learn from both success and failure. After a product launch, the company collects feedback from the customer's sales team to help guide future business.

The business provides quality vehicles and equipment for sales. Example Provide your salespeople with quality sales information, research and competitive information. Collaboration encourages creativity and innovation. Example Strategy, sales, and marketing personnel work together to explore new ideas or applications.

Strategic Collaboration

Meetings bring the sales and marketing teams together regularly to prepare plans, set goals, and share hand Example a three-month workshop where two groups meet and develop plans together. Identify key performance indicators (KPIs) relevant to both groups.

These KPIs often include conversion rate, customer lifetime value, or revenue from marketing campaigns. Invest in tools that support collaboration, such as collaborative work management and CRM systems.

Example Use a CRM system to allow your sales and marketing teams to track interactions with potential and existing customers. Recognize shared achievements and celebrate milestones within the team. If marketing success translates into sales, recognize your team's efforts. Collaboration is more than just working together. It's about building relationships by leveraging each other's strengths. By fostering a culture of collaboration, companies can accelerate growth, improve customer experience, and increase revenue.

CHAPTER 6

Executing Effective Sales and Marketing Plan.

Sales and marketing plan is about how your business will attract, engage, and convert people to patronize your goods and services. It includes the goals, strategies, and metrics of your sales and marketing teams and how they work together to achieve your business goals. Sales and Marketing Management cover managing a sales team, making sales decisions, deciding on sales strategies, setting sales goals and deciding how to achieve the brand plan. Before your business starts selling products and services, consider the legal and fair sales, pricing, warranty, deposit and return, etc.

Sales and marketing advice will help you meet your customers' needs and protect you and your business from police fines, fines, injunctions and other risks.

Creating a good sales and marketing strategy is crucial to the growth of your business because it helps you:

- Increase your brand awareness and business reputation.
- By creating and delivering content that is relevant and relevant to your audience, you establish yourself as a reliable and trustworthy source of information and solutions.
- Generate more leads and grow your sales pipeline. By using effective and efficient channels and strategies to reach and interact with potential customers.

To capture Customers interests to make decision on purchase:

- Improve your customer experience and satisfaction.
- By improving your sales and marketing teams, you can effectively communicate and interact with your customers and deliver on your promises and services.
- Set clear and measurable goals for your sales and marketing teams, to track and monitor your progress and performance.
- Maintain and expand the existing customer base. By caring and delighting your existing customers, you can increase their loyalty and retention and encourage them to buy more from you or recommend you to others.

Competition may infiltrate the market, or technology may disrupt the way customers want to receive similar products and services. So, put downpour tools for a moment and focus on your marketing strategy.

The keys to marketing are identifying customer needs and developing solutions to meet those needs. Getting products and services right and then delivering them to your customers is essential to increasing sales and growing your business. Therefore, it is important to remain customer-centric and make your business and brand stand out from the crowd. But first, before you jump into printing flyers or advertising, it's a good idea to take some time to think about your strategy and plan your activities.

Not having a strategy or plan can mean you don't achieve what you want and risk wasting time and money.

A useful framework for understanding marketing is known as the "7Ps."

This will help you consider what makes up your marketing mix. It is something that is created or provided to meet the needs of the customer.

The 7P's of Marketing

Price, pricing strategy and how customers pay for your product or service.

The place is where your product or service is produced, discovered, distributed, sold and supported. This may be a physical or a digital entity.

Promotion is a way to communicate products and services to target customers to encourage them to purchase.

The **people** stand for those who work in your business, including you.

The **processes** and activities involved in delivering your product or service. This means you'll make it easier for your customers to do business with you.

This includes physical space, the look and feel of your brand, and ratings and reviews and more.

Below is a breakdown of the six stages of marketing strategy development.

1. *Know your current situation.* This includes understanding the market and knowing the strengths and weaknesses of your business.

2. *Set marketing goals*: These are clear, realistic and measurable goals.

3. *Define your target segments.* In other words, who are your customers and do you understand their current and future needs?

4. *Perform a competitive analysis to understand your competitors* and learn how you can create a sustainable competitive advantage.

5. *Define your brand positioning.* It's about the goals of your business, *what you want to be known for and your place in the hearts and minds of your customers.*

6. *Identify your priorities*. Thinking through the first five steps should help you to understand how you should priorities the marketing programs

CHAPTER 7

Implementing the Sales Strategy

A sales strategy is a plan, tool or strategy that you or your sales team can use to achieve your sales goals. This strategy sets clear goals and provides guidelines for you or your sales team to follow. *These strategies may focus on generating sales, attracting more customers, or marketing your products to all potential customers.* Effective selling ensures that sales teams achieve their goals. There are many strategies salespeople can use when pitching to a customer, business, or company; all of which help motivate buyers to buy what you're selling. There are many strategies you can use, including how to: retain existing customers, attract new customers, and sell more products to existing customers (such as upselling).

Strategies help your salespeople achieve realistic sales goals and are generally aligned with your business strategy. You can help salespeople achieve their goals by generating qualified leads and awareness through marketing campaigns. AIDA's effective selling model supports and meets the intellectual and creative needs of our customers.

The AIDA model describes 4 sales processes:
- ✓ Attract customer satisfaction
- ✓ Increase customer satisfaction
- ✓ Create customer demand for the product
- ✓ Drive customer business and supplies.

Some sales experts today suggest modifying the old AIDA model and adding (persuasion) and (satisfaction) to make online marketing easier today. This change recognizes the importance of customers' trust and satisfaction in the products they choose.

AIDA technology is not just for sale. The technology can also be used in advertising and marketing campaigns.

A sales strategy is a plan to help your sales team achieve sales goals.

This means how your team responds to your product or service, how you define and focus on quality, and how you communicate your goals. Selling also includes popular sales techniques and techniques such as persuasion, qualification, presentation, negotiation, and closing.

A sales strategy can help you:

Align your sales team with your business goals and vision. Increase your sales and performance, improve your sales and investments, increase your customer satisfaction and trust and gain a competitive advantage.

The steps in creating a sales strategy are:

1. Determine your sales goals
2. Determine your market and competitors
3. Determine the characteristics of your ideal customers and your customers' behavior.
4. Create your quotes and sales specifications
5. Choose your sales pipeline and methods.
6. Create your sales process and pipeline.
7. Set your sales quotas and payment plans.
8. Train and train your team sales.
9. Track and measure your sales

sales strategy for sales team

Determine the target audience for your business.

So, who are the customers who benefit from this product or service? What are their needs, problems, goals and interests? How do you reach and communicate with them? Please describe your business and competitors.

What are your competing products or services? How do they define themselves and how do they differ? What are the pros and cons? How can you stand out from the crowd and offer something unique or valuable?

Create pricing and sales information for your products or services.

What is the key benefiting your product or service provides to your customers? How does it solve a problem or help you achieve a goal?

Do you take a different approach to selling and marketing your products or services? How can we convey this message clearly and persuasively? How will you distribute and promote your product to your target audience? Will you be using online platforms such as social media, email marketing, or online shopping? Will you use it offline, in stores, at events or through word of mouth?

Effective Strategies to close deal and make sales

Improve sales and promotion processes.

Customers will know what steps they need to take to purchase your product. How do you guide them through each stage of the buyer's journey (awareness, interest, consideration, decision, action)? What tools and strategies will you use to attract, grow, convert, and retain customers?

Analyze sales quotas and pricing plans for each product.

How much and when do you want to sell it? How will you measure and track sales and progress? How will you reward yourself or your team for meeting your sales goals?

Train yourself and your team.

How can you increase sales and awareness of the products you sell? What best practices and lessons can we learn from other successful companies?

How do you get feedback and support from colleagues, coaches, and mentors?

Track and measure sales made

How will you review and rate our products and recommendations? What key indicators and indicators will you use to measure sales and performance?

How do you identify and resolve discrepancies or problems in sales or operations? How can we celebrate success and learn from failure? Your target audience is one of the most important aspects of your sales strategy. Because it determines who you sell to and how you reach them.

Determine your target audience when developing a sales strategy.

Define your ideal customer Profile (ICP). This is a description of the customers most likely to buy your product or service based on criteria such as industry, size, location, budget, needs, brand goals, and issues.

You can create an ICP using information from existing customers, market research, or industry reports.

Well-informed the buyers

It is the process by which a customer becomes aware of your product or service and makes a purchase decision. You must define stages and touch points based on the content and message you want to convey at each stage and impress customers.

Select a sales method

This is a way to distribute and promote your product or service to your target audience.

You need to think about the best way to communicate with customers, including online platforms, offline, recommendations, partnerships, and events.

You need to decide which sales method (inbound, outbound, or hybrid) is best for your product or service.

Create sales processes and sales funnels.

The Steps your sales team should take to convert leads into actual customers. You need to define processes and activities for each stage of the pipeline: decision, review, presentation, discussion, and closing. You also need to develop tools, measure management, and measure sales. A unique selling proposition is a unique feature that makes your product or service stands out from the competition.

To create a good product, you need to decide:

Target Market: Who is your ideal customer and what are their needs, problems, and goals?

Your solution: Does your product or service solve your customer's problem or help them achieve their goal?

Your Value: What value do you provide to your customers and how do you measure it? What is different from other companies? What makes you special?

To increase sales, you need to focus on:

Your strengths: What do you do better than others in the market?

Your Evidence: How do you prove your worth through facts, evidence, or statements?

Promise: What facts and message do you want to convey to your customers?

A proposition is a statement that explains the benefits a product or service will provide to customers and differentiates it from other products or services on the market. This is a valuable promise to our customers.

Unique Selling Point (USP) is a phrase that describes the unique value of a product or service and differentiates it from competitors.

Sales are divided into two categories: direct sales and indirect sales

Direct sales channels are sales made directly to customers. The company Direct sales team communicate directly with customers. B2B companies often use this type of selling. Your company sells products or services online through its own website or app.

Indirect selling sells products to consumers through Intermediaries. Company sells products in physical stores or online stores and then resells them to customers. This allows you to distribute your products widely and promote your store and customers. Your company sells products to distributors or dealers, who then sell the products to retailers or consumers. This allows you to reach new markets and reduce logistics costs.

Your company pays other businesses or businesses to sell your products or services to customers. This helps you generate leads and increase sales conversion rates. To create a good presentation, you need to think about your product or service, your target audience, your competitors, and your resource. Research your business and your customers' interests. Find out where your prospects are looking for solutions, what channels they trust, and what influences their purchasing decisions. Identify competitors and identify gaps or opportunities. Find out what channels your competitors use, how they work, and what their strengths and weaknesses are. Find ways to differentiate your product or reach underserved segments. Evaluate the suitability and value of your product or service.

Evaluate how well your product or service fits into each sales line, how much each sales line sells for, and how much revenue and profit each sales line can generate

Measure channel performance and customer satisfaction. Try different sales channels and track sales metrics like leads, conversion rates, and retention rates. A sales strategy is a plan to reach and sell to customers through various channels such as direct sales, distributors, distributors, or online platforms. A good sales strategy can help you expand your reach, increase sales, and reduce costs.

Case Study

Transforming the struggling Retail chain.

Background and Issues

Company: A medium-sized retail chain with several stores in various cities.

Problem:

The retail industry is facing fierce competition, declining foot traffic and declining profits. The company struggled to survive.

1. Sales stagnated and customer loyalty.
2. Outdated systems of inventory management and customer service became difficult.
3. Delays in restocking lead to stockouts and customer complaints.
4. High operating cost: Rent, utilities, and labor costs were eating into profits.

Strategy Applied

1. Customer-centric approach

Problem Solved: The company conducted extensive market research to understand customer preferences, pain points, and purchasing behavior.

 solution: A loyalty program with individual discounts and personal recommendations has been implemented.

In-Store Experience: Updated store layout, trained staff and introduction of interactive displays.

2. Omnichannel Integration: Seamlessly connect of online and offline channels for a customer experience.

Technical Update: Troubleshoots automated systems reduce efficiency and customer satisfaction.

Solution

POS System: Updated to the latest POS system to speed up transactions.

Inventory Management: Real-time inventory tracking has been implemented to prevent out of stock.

E-commerce platform: We launched an e-commerce website to increase online sales.

3. Supply Chain Optimization

Problem:

Inefficient supply chain was causing delays and impacting customer satisfaction.

solution

Supplier Collaboration: Strengthen relationships with suppliers to ensure on-time delivery.

Centralized Warehouse: Integrated inventory management for better control.

Automatic Reorder: Set an automatic reorder trigger to prevent you from running out of stock.

Cost savings- Problem Solved: High operating costs were eating into profits

Energy Efficiency: Energy saving measures have been implemented in the stores.

5. Job Optimization:

A workforce that is cross-trained to perform a variety of roles.

Lease Negotiation: Renegotiate lease terms to reduce lease costs. Results and Impact

Sales Growth: Sales increased 20% over 12 months thanks to improved customer service and targeted marketing.

Profitability: Increased profitability with a 15% reduction in operating costs.

Customer Satisfaction: Net Promoter Score (NPS) increased from market share. Retailers have gained market share by providing a seamless shopping experience across multiple channels.

Takeout

Holistic approach: Combining customer focus, technology, supply chain optimization and cost reduction is essential.

Adaptive: Constantly monitor trends and adjust your strategy to stay competitive.

Collaboration: We work closely with our suppliers, employees and customers to achieve mutual success.

This case study shows how strategic alignment, innovation, and relentless execution can transform a struggling business into a thriving business.

CHAPTER 8

Management of the Sales Department

The management of the Sales department entails everything that matters in the department and account for the numbers. Anything that comes into play in the department should not ignore. From the strategies to team. Get to know your target customers and their needs, preferences and buying habits. This will help you choose the best pipe for each area. Examine your current sales funnel and its effectiveness. Identify the strengths, weaknesses, opportunities, and threats of each pipeline and identify any gaps or overlaps in approaches.

Find and select a partner who can help you attract customers. The sales process is the steps a salesperson takes to follow a prospect from contact to purchase.

A sales pipeline is a visual representation of the sales process that shows where each prospect is in the buying process. However, what needs to be done to move to the next stage.

Creation of sales process and sales pipeline

Define the stages

Create a sales process based on your business, products and customer needs. For example, you might have phases such as leadership, communication, qualification, demo, outsourcing, and close/win or close/fail. Check the procedures and activities for each stage, such as appropriate questions, presentation type, proposal and follow-up.

Choose a sales tool or CRM software that allows you to create and manage pipelines, track deals, and measure performance.

Fill your lead funnel through a variety of sources, including referrals, online marketing, cold calling, and social media. Monitor and improve your sales funnel by analyzing conversion rates, impact metrics, referral rates, and sales forecasts. Use this information to identify conflicts, improve your sales strategy, and achieve your sales goals.

A sales funnel is a way to track and manage a buyer's progress from first contact to final purchase.

This allows salespeople to plan and forecast higher-than-expected profits. Sales funnel typically consists of several stages, including research, analysis, presentation, negotiation, and closing. Each step has its own processes and tasks to move to the next step or exit the pipeline. You can use a sales funnel tool or CRM software like Sales force to create and manage your sales funnels. These tools help sellers track deals, advance projects, and measure performance. Using sales funnels can benefit you and your sales team.

Clear conversations

Understand where each prospect is in their buying journey and what you need to do to take them to the next level. This will help you prioritize your tasks and focus on your best moments.

Measure team performance

Track how well each salesperson generates revenue, closes sales, and generates revenue. You can also identify areas that need improvement and provide feedback and recommendations.

Sales Forecast

You can predict future sales based on the quantity and value of products in your sales funnel. You can adjust your sales strategy and goals based on data and trends in your sales funnel. Sales Funnels are powerful tools that help you increase sales, sales, and productivity.

Creating the sales funnel.

Assign sales levels based on business, product, and customer requirements. For example, you might have stages like Lead, Contact, Qualification, Demonstration, Outsource, Close / Success, or Close. Review step-by-step procedures and activities, including relevant questions, presentation types, contract terms, follow-up actions, etc. Choose a sales tool or CRM software that allows you to create and manage your sales pipeline, track deals, and measure performance.

Monitor and optimize your sales funnel by analyzing conversion rates, impact metrics, referral rates, and sales forecasts. Use this information to identify conflicts, improve your sales strategy, and achieve your sales goals. Creating a sales and payment plan is a complex task that involves balancing company's and seller's benefits as well as coordinating support with sales and goals. Here are some steps to follow: Choose metrics that reflect the value and performance of your sales team, such as monthly revenue (MRR), annual contract value (ACV), or customer value (CLV). Set realistic goals for the quotas each salesperson can achieve based on their role, experience, and advertising and marketing capabilities. You can use historical data, business model, and growth to determine quota levels. Select the average annual salary or variable annual salary payment method.

The average salary should cover the salesperson's living expenses, and commissions should compensate for meeting or exceeding goals. A rule of thumb is to split fixed and variable costs 50/50, but this will vary depending on your business, products and sales. Establish fee structures and payment plans. You can calculate your income using a variety of methods, including flat fees, quota percentages, and profit percentages. Boosters, bonuses, or incentives can be used to encourage salespeople to exceed quotas or sell products or services.

Payment should be made as soon as possible after the sale, preferably monthly or quarterly.
Communicate sales quotas and payment plans clearly and transparently to the sales team.

Request feedback and respond to the seller's questions or comments. Regularly monitor and evaluate sales plans and payment plans.

Use data and analytics to track your sales team's progress and results and identify issues or gaps in your plan. Adjust plans as needed to reflect changes in the market, inventory or sales.

Focus on the health and mental well-being of your delegation and lead them with acceptance and confidence. Customize training to fit each salesperson's needs, skills and skills. Use data and metrics to set goals and strategies and track sales and performance. Use tools and techniques to analyze sales and identify areas for improvement. It encourages continuous learning and improvement and provides opportunities for practice and feedback. - Celebrate success and achievements and reward good behavior and results. Tracking and measuring sales is important for developing your sales strategy and achieving your goals.

Tactics to win the team
Define sales and key performance indicators.

This data measures the effectiveness of your sales team and salespeople. You should choose metrics that align with your sales goals and reflect sales performance, such as sales, average order value, conversion rate, and customer retention rate. Collect and analyze sales data. You can track and visualize your sales performance using a variety of tools and methods, such as spreadsheets. You need to find patterns, trends, and insights that will help you understand your sales and identify your strengths and weaknesses. Providing advice and training to the sales team. Based on the sales analysis, suggestions and recommendations should be made to improve the sales force, their behavior, and their results. Their successes and achievements should be celebrated and rewarded.

Make changes and track your progress.

You should use sales analysis to inform your sales strategies and plans and make adjustments as needed. You need to track the impact of changes on sales and measure the results. Inside sales and outside sales are two strategies that can help you generate leads, close deals, and grow your business. But they have different advantages and disadvantages, and which one is best for your business depends on many factors.

CHAPTER 9

Getting Customers Trust and Loyalty

You need to be able to provide your customers with important information and updates via email, phone, or social media. You must respond and contact customers using their preferred method of communication.

Provide excellent customer service and support.

You must provide high-quality products and services that meet or exceed your customers' needs and leave them satisfied and happy with your company. Provide support and assistance to customers and resolve their problems quickly and efficiently. Show your gratitude and reward loyalty. You should thank your customers for their cooperation and feedback and express your gratitude.

You should reward your loyal customers with incentives, discounts, or freebies and encourage them to recommend your company to other. Promote your product well and get reviews.

Practice listening and sharing what you know.

 You should listen carefully to your customers' questions, concerns, and suggestions and try to understand their needs and expectations. You will demonstrate your experience and confidence and propose solutions that meet the client's goals.

Be honest and transparent with your customers.

You must understand and adhere to the Company's values, policies and procedures and refrain from making any negative advertisements or misrepresentations. We must admit our mistakes, take responsibility and if necessary, apologize and make compensation.

Tips to promote your product and its popularity

You need to explain what your product is, what it does, and how it helps your customers. It must also be able to communicate the value of your product and how it differs from the competition. Understand your buyer. You must be able to identify and understand the various aspects, needs, goals and pain points of your target customers. You need to adapt your voice to each person's situation, use words and sounds that work for them, and focus on the outcomes that matter most to them. Be prepared for various attacks. You need to be able to anticipate and address the most common objections your customers may face, including price, time, cost, and competitors. Problem Solving requires the use of problem-focused principles such as "listening, exploring, learning, and responding.

Sales innovation for offerings

Sales innovation is the process of creating and implementing new or improved ways of selling your products or services to your customers. Sales innovation can help you differentiate yourself from your competitors, increase your customer satisfaction and loyalty, and boost your revenue and growth[12].

Leveraging technology to drive sales innovation and improve offerings.

Technology can help you collect and analyze data on customer behavior, market trends, and internal processes, and use it to gain insights and generate new ideas. Technology can also help you create seamless and personalized customer experiences, embed relevant services in the customer journey, and enhance your product portfolio.

Some examples are: building relationships via social media, embedding you in local communities, trying a customer loyalty program, using customer-centric sales techniques, and trying a sales liaison. You can explain how these examples can help you reach new markets, customers, and channels, and increase your sales performance and efficiency.

CHAPTER 10

Measuring Your Sales

Measuring sales is important for many reasons and is a must because it great a picture of your sales activities.

First, it helps you measure how well you're meeting your sales goals. Secondly, it helps you identify your strengths and weaknesses, as well as areas for improvement. Third, it helps you make informed decisions and take necessary actions to improve your sales strategies and ideas. You must use effective sales metrics and metrics to measure your sales results. These are quantitative and qualitative measures that affect your sales and profits.

Some of the most important metrics and sales metrics are:

Revenue

This is the revenue you make from your sales. It is calculated by multiplying the number of products sold and the average sales price. Revenue is an important indicator of sales growth and market share.

Profit

It is the money you get after deducting costs and expenses from your sales. It is calculated by subtracting all costs and expenses from total revenue. Revenue is an important indicator of your sales profitability and efficiency.

Conversion and retention rate

It is calculated by dividing the number of customers by potential customers. Conversion rate is an important indicator of effective and efficient sales. Retention rate is an important indicator of customer satisfaction and loyalty.

Satisfaction

How happy and satisfied your customers are with your products, services and interactions. It is evaluated through observation, feedback, analysis, evaluation and recommendations. Satisfaction is an important indicator of customer value and feedback. You can measure and evaluate your sales using these sales metrics and metrics. You can compare your results with your goals, benchmarks, and competitors. This will help you identify trends, opportunities and threats and take appropriate action to increase your sales and profits.

Case Study

Innovative Strategies to penetrate deep into the markets

The fascinating journey of Melanie Perkins, the co-founder and CEO of Canva, and the significant impact she has made through her innovative business strategies to penetrate deep into the markets.

Background of Canva:

Canva, a graphic design platform, was launched in 2013 by Melanie Perkins, along with co-founders-Cliff Obrecht and Cameron Adams. Melanie's vision was born out of her observation of the complexities involved in using traditional design software.

While teaching design at a university, she recognized the steep learning curve and the inaccessibility of design tools for the average person.

This led to the idea of creating a platform that simplified design, making it accessible to everyone, regardless of their design skills.

Canva's mission is to empower everyone to design, believing that design should be simple, enjoyable, and accessible.

Canva's Journey:

From Idea to Reality:

Melanie and Cliff's first venture, Fusion Books, an online tool for designing school yearbooks, laid the groundwork for Canva. Canva went live in 2013 with an intuitive drag-and-drop interface, a vast library of templates, and accessibility across devices. The platform aims to democratize design, allowing anyone to create beautiful designs without prior experience.

Key Features of Canva:

   1. *Design Templates:*

Canva offers a wide range of customizable templates for various design needs.

   2. *Collaboration Tools:*

Users can collaborate on designs in real-time, making teamwork seamless.

   3. *Capabilities:*

Canva allows users to personalize templates, fonts, colors, and layouts.

   4. *Brand Kit:*

Businesses can maintain consistent branding across designs.

   5. *Animation and Video Editing*:

Canva expanded into video content Planner: Helps users schedule and organize social media posts.

   6. *Integrations*:

Canva integrates with other tools and platforms.

7. *Learning Resources:*

Provides tutorials and educational content.

8. *Canva Magic Studio*:

A creative space for experimentation.

Canva's Growth Strategy:

Focused Targeting:

Canva identified its niche audience and tailored its product to their needs.

User-Focused Marketing Approach:

Canva prioritized user feedback and continuously improved its features.

Product-Led Growth:

The power of simplicity, network effects, and community building drove organic growth.

International Expansion:

Canva expanded globally, reaching millions of users worldwide.

Impact on Graphic Design:

-Canva disrupted the design software market by making design accessible to non-designers.

Challenges included competition, adapting to changing user needs, scaling the platform, and maintaining innovation.

Canva's monetization strategy, talent acquisition, and retention were critical areas of focus.

Learnings from Canva:

1. *User-Centric Product Development*:

Canva's success lies in understanding user pain points and addressing them.

2. *The Power of Simplicity:*

Canva's intuitive interface made design accessible.

3. *Leveraging Network Effects:*

Collaborative features encourage user engagement.

4. *Innovation*:

Canva consistently adds new features and tools.

5. *Building:*

Canva's active community contributes to its growth.

6. *Focused Design:*

Prioritizing user experience drives Canva's success. = *Melanie Perkins' vision and Canva's impact on the design world demonstrate the power of simplicity, accessibility, and community-driven growth.*

CONCLUSIONS

The market is constantly changing and evolving and so should your business. To succeed in today's competitive and dynamic environment, you need to be versatile, innovative and customer-centric. You also need to collaborate with other businesses that share your vision and values, and can complement your strengths and weaknesses. By combining forces with other businesses, you can create a powerful network that can help you go deep into the market and achieve maximum impact. You can leverage each other's resources, expertise, and insights, and create synergies that will benefit all parties involved. You can also create value for your customers, and offer them more value, variety, and convenience. To make this happen, you need to discuss topics that are relevant and important for your market, such as customer needs, preferences, market trends and opportunities, competitive analysis and differentiation, marketing strategies and tactics, performance measurement and improvement. You need to communicate openly, honestly, and respectfully, and listen to each other's feedback and suggestions. You also need to align your goals, expectations, and responsibilities, and establish clear and mutually beneficial agreements. By doing so, you will be able to create a win-win situation for your business, your partners, and your customers. You will be able to deepen your market penetration, expand your market reach, increase your market share, and enhance your market reputation. You will also be able to grow your sales, profits, customer loyalty, and achieve your business objectives.

See you at the top …. Great Business Leader

www.ingramcontent.com/pod-product-compliance
Lightning Source LLC
Chambersburg PA
CBHW071935210526
45479CB00002B/687